TRUCKER

written and photographed by

Hope Herman Wurmfeld

MACMILLAN PUBLISHING COMPANY
NEW YORK

COLLIER MACMILLAN PUBLISHERS
LONDON

By the same author

Boatbuilder

Many thanks to Phil and Cathy Marcum and their entire family,
of Oneida, Tennessee, and to the children in Hillary Markum's
first-grade class at the Burchfield School.

Macmillan Publishing Company
866 Third Avenue, New York, NY 10022
Collier Macmillan Canada, Inc.
First Edition
Printed in the United States of America

10 9 8 7 6 5 4 3 2 1

The text of this book is set in 14 point Stempel Garamond.
The illustrations are black-and-white photographs reproduced in halftone.

Library of Congress Cataloging-in-Publication Data
Wurmfeld, Hope Herman.
Trucker / written and photographed by Hope Herman Wurmfeld.—1st ed.   p.   cm.
Summary: Describes the duties, responsibilities, route, and cargo of a
long-distance truck driver as he hauls lumber, steel, or produce
from Canada to Florida in his tractor trailer.
ISBN 0–02–793581–7
1. Truck driving—Juvenile literature. [1. Truck driving.
2. Occupations.] I. Title.
TL230.15.W87 1990 388.4′1324—dc20   89–13296   CIP   AC

To my father,
Charles H. Herman

It is early October, but the Tennessee landscape is still green with summer. Box elders and sugar maples are only now beginning to turn golden.

Driving through the foothills of the Cumberland Mountains on I-75, Phil Marcum pulls his Kenworth eighteen-wheeler over to the right-hand lane to make room for faster-moving vehicles that would like to pass.

Phil Marcum is a trucker who owns and operates his own rig: a rebuilt tractor trailer, vintage 1968. He hauls lumber, steel, or produce on a north-south route from Canada to Florida, and sometimes drives almost three thousand miles a week before going home for the weekend.

As Phil approaches the Kentucky state line, he is close to where he lives in Oneida, Tennessee. He honks the horn and sends up puffs of smoke for good luck when he passes the exit off I-75 that would take him home.

Phil misses his family when he's on the road. But there is no time for stopping. He is hauling fifty thousand pounds of lumber that is expected in Ohio by tomorrow morning. He hopes to make it home in time for his daughters' basketball game Friday night.

Phil changes gears as he starts up Jellico Mountain over the state line into Kentucky. There are thirteen gears that he uses every time he starts the truck and fourteen dials on the dashboard to tell him how the truck is doing. There are gauges for oil temperature, water temperature, oil pressure, air pressure, truck speed (speedometer), engine speed (rpm indicator), and time.

Phil's rig consists of a flatbed for the load and a cab with an engine to pull it. His cab is called a conventional because the motor is in front, the way it is in a car. Some cabs have the motor directly beneath the driver's seat; this kind is called a cab-over.

    Many trucks are climbing the long hill out of Tennessee to points north. Phil is in constant communication with the rigs around him as he drives. When a truck passes, Phil flashes the lights that are mounted on the roof of his cab to signal to the other driver that he has fully cleared Phil's rig and can move into the slower lane again.

On the CB he hears, "Hey, Rocky Top! Come in, Rocky Top! Can you read me, Rocky Top?" Some people say Rocky Top is a peak in the mountains of Tennessee and can also mean a person from Tennessee.

Drivers often have a special name, called a handle, that they use on their CB radios. Usually the name is something personal. Phil is sometimes called Legs, because he's tall, or Easy Rider, from his motorcycle days when he rode a Harley Davidson.

Phil checks in. "Rocky Top here. What's happenin'?"

"Hey, old buddy! Listen up! You got trouble in your northbound lane. Looks like a tractor trailer's off the road. Better check it out at the next stop."

Although Phil is still too far away to see it, just ahead traffic is backed up for ten miles.

Phil maneuvers into the nearest truck stop. Thirty or forty big rigs have already pulled in. Their engines are idling while the drivers decide whether to risk going around.

Phil sits silently for several minutes, his elbows resting on his knees, his hands on the wheel.

From the CB a voice says, "I'm goin' round. What're you doin', Tennessee?"

"I think I'm gonna wait for 'em to clear the road," Phil answers.

"It's about thirty miles," says the voice on the CB. "But the way they're talkin', this could take all night. I don't know if I can get this set of joints through these hills, but I'm gonna give it a try. I got a load to deliver."

"Yeah, well, I think I'll take a nap," Phil answers. "Good luck, Colorado."

Colorado revs his engine and heads out into the night.

Phil climbs into the bunk of his conventional and stretches out. He hopes to be under way again in two hours.

Many drivers have made the same decision. Trucks are pulling in and making a huge circle, like wagon trains encamped for the night, around the central facilities of the truck stop.

It is after midnight when Phil's alarm clock awakens him. The truck stop is almost deserted now. The wreck has been cleared. The CB is quiet. It's time to hit the road.

What happened up there with the tractor trailer? Phil doesn't know. The driver might have fallen asleep at the wheel. He might have braked too fast going downhill. The grade down Jellico Mountain isn't as steep as the one on Monteagle, another long hill that is often on Phil's route, but it can be difficult if the weather is bad or if a driver is tired.

Phil has been driving for sixteen years and has never had an accident. He rarely gets a flat. He watches the Kenworth carefully, for he knows his life depends on it.

Early morning in Ohio. Phil stops for breakfast at a diner. He thinks about calling home, but realizes that it's too early. His family won't get up for at least another hour. Phil orders pancakes, eggs, and tea.

Back to the truck and I-75. He drives for an hour and stops for fuel somewhere between Dayton and Toledo.

The truck holds five hundred gallons of diesel and diesel weighs about seven pounds a gallon. When the truck is loaded, Phil runs close to empty. He doesn't want to exceed the legal-load limit for his rig, which is about eighty thousand pounds.

Fuel is one of a driver's biggest expenses. Diesel costs about ninety-seven cents a gallon in some places, but the truck only gets five miles to the gallon.

After the truck has been refueled, Phil washes down the entire rig with a large hose. He uses blackener on the tires and a feather duster on the cab. He isn't the only trucker engaged in this activity.

Some people say that the bigger, shinier, better-looking the rig, the more responsible the driver. Most drivers take pride in their machines and try hard to keep them looking good.

By late morning Phil delivers the load of lumber to the Neowood Products Company in Alvada, Ohio. The lumber is removed from the rig by a worker with a forklift. From Alvada, Phil will do what drivers call deadheading. He'll drive the truck empty to pick up his next load in Canada.

As he drives he sees shopping malls, factories, motels, and fast-food chains. Phil makes this trip twice a week and sometimes more often. It's all part of the job.

Music helps him to get down the road. Phil listens to the radio or to his tape deck. He likes rock and roll and the blues sound.

Passing through Detroit he hears on the CB that the bridge into Canada is backed up.

A small sign says TO CANADA—BRIDGE. The Ambassador Bridge crosses into Canada and spans the Detroit River. Lake Erie and Lake St. Clair lie on either side. Two hundred miles to the east is Niagara Falls.

The customs inspector on the Canadian side asks for the truck's documents. He asks if Phil is an American citizen and if he has anything to declare.

The inspector asks very specifically whether he is carrying handguns, alcohol, or drugs. Phil answers that he is an American citizen, and no, he has nothing to declare and is not carrying anything illegal. The inspector waves him on.

A couple of times Phil has been pulled over and the border patrol has gone through the entire rig. They even asked him to take his shoes off. You never know, says Phil, when they are going to do that.

Windsor, Ontario. It is late afternoon and Phil is at the lumberyard loading up. As soon as he makes his delivery in Ohio tomorrow morning, he'll be ready to head home. He wants to be on time for his daughters' basketball game Friday night.

It's midnight when Phil pulls the rig into his daddy's farm. He parks at the farm because the truck is too large to maneuver the narrow road to his own place. The game is long over.

Phil's house is quiet. He tiptoes in, not wanting to wake anyone. The girls have left him a note: "Sorry you missed the game. We missed you, Dad. Love, Us. P.S. We won, 48 to 12."

He sits on the sofa and closes his eyes for a moment. Tomorrow we'll go horseback riding at the farm, he thinks. We'll saddle up a couple of horses and go for a ride.

Phil lives with his wife, Cathy, and their four daughters. The oldest, Casey, will graduate from high school in the spring. The middle two, Lisa and Nicole, are all-state basketball champions. Their team is the best in the state. Hillary, who wants to be a truck driver when she grows up, is the youngest. Phil smiles to himself when he thinks about Hillary. Hillary is wise beyond her years and is reading after only a month in first grade.

Phil does not wake up early on Saturday morning. When he's home, he needs to catch up on sleep. That afternoon everyone climbs into the Ford pickup truck to go to Grandpa's. Granddaddy Marcum's place is only a stone's throw from where Phil lives. At one time it had been one large farm. Now Phil and his brother and sister each have a part of the land that had been the original homestead.

Lisa and Nicole bring saddles and blanket pads out of the barn. They like to ride the Tennessee walking horse and the old chestnut mare.

They notice that the walking horse has a split hoof, but decide that it will be all right to ride her in the pasture.

Grandpa has been working on the roof of the barn. He is making a large overhang so that dry grain and hay can be left out for the cattle in winter. Phil and his dad sit with Hillary and talk about the construction.

Phil loves cars, especially old ones. The truth is that on any given day the Marcums have about a dozen cars around their house. Phil works on them when he's home.

Sunday is family day at the Marcums, and everyone has come to Phil and Cathy's house. There are cars everywhere. Almost as many cars as Phil's truck has wheels.

Everyone comes in with food for sharing and jokes and the latest stories from the week.

"How do you spell hard water with only three letters?" Phil asks. Nobody knows.

"I-C-E, you all." Phil laughs.

"Oh, Daddy. That's awful." Lisa and Nicole groan.

Hamburgers and hot dogs are cooking on the grill.

After dessert it's time for kickball, the kids against the grown-ups. They play to win. Phil is on the sofa trying to relax, but not for long. Hillary comes in and pulls him outside to play.

Everyone helps to decide where the bases will go: one large tree for third and piles of leaves for first and second bases and for home plate.

Phil pitches for the grown-up team. He's big, fast, and accurate. If Phil has the ball and you're running to base, you're going to be out. That ball is going to hit you. Phil doesn't miss.

The game ends in a draw because no one can find the bases; they have become part of the ground cover of leaves.

Built into a trucker's schedule is the moment when it's time to go—to get under way again.

Late Sunday afternoon Phil checks the truck to make sure that everything is in good working order for the drive south. He stocks fresh shirts, socks, jeans, clean sheets for his bunk bed, and a Thermos for cold drinks.

In spring Phil rides a different route. He deadheads down to Immokalee, Florida, ninety miles northwest of Miami to pick up a load of watermelons. He drives south nine hundred miles in eighteen hours. Approaching Monteagle in southern Tennessee, a large sign says MOUNTAIN GRADE 4.5%. USE LOWER GEAR NEXT 5 MILES. A row of lights across the road read either red, yellow, or green. They are for speed control based on weather conditions and traffic.

There is a safety feature on Monteagle called a cutaway ramp—a spur of road cut at points along a downhill grade on the right of the roadway. The ramp leads off the main road and ends in a sand pit that goes uphill. If a truck gets into trouble and can't slow down, the driver can pull off into the cutaway and know that his truck will stop.

A weigh station is coming up. Phil drives over the scales in the ground and is not waved through. A yellow light flashes telling him to pull over. The inspectors are looking at the truck in front of his. Phil's will be next.

Phil is concerned about the inspection. He gets out of the rig with his papers. The inspectors look at the physical condition of the truck and at the log.

A trucker's log is an outline of his trip and a record of how he spends his time. The federal government has strict regulations. A driver is supposed to drive no more than ten hours a day, to sleep eight hours, and to spend the other six hours relaxing. The activities may be broken up in different ways, but the hours must add up to twenty-four.

Phil's log is in order, but the inspectors are concerned about some of the tires. Phil will have them checked as soon as he gets home. He needs eighteen good wheels for safety and efficiency. He'll replace them next weekend in Tennessee.

Again on I-75 Phil passes the Russell Cave National Monument and the Tennessee River. Bluegrass guitar plays on the radio.

The road curves and a sign reads WELCOME TO GEORGIA, THE STATE OF ADVENTURE, CAVES, WHITE WATER, PEACHES, AND PEANUTS. Someday, Phil thinks, he would like to try caving or white-water rafting on the Tennessee River with his family.

There are still three hundred and fifty miles to drive through Georgia. That's seven hours of driving. Then there's another three hundred miles to the end of Florida.

For each state that a driver passes through, a license plate or fuel sticker is required. The plate or sticker provides a record of the kinds of vehicles regularly using the roads and a way of collecting money for keeping the roads in shape. The cost varies from forty to four hundred dollars, depending on the state.

Phil stops for fuel and a nap about fifty miles south of Atlanta. He fills up with 280 gallons of diesel. Here it's ninety-five cents a gallon, and he pays by check. He doesn't use credit cards. Phil says he gets a better price with checks or cash.

After many hours of driving Phil reaches Florida. He turns off I-75 to a smaller, yellow-lined road, U.S. 27. There are many citrus trees—orange and lemon—in all stages of growth.

As thunderclouds form overhead, Phil watches the sky and listens for a weather forecast. Watermelons can't be picked if it rains. Sometimes drivers wait around Immokalee for a week until the rain stops.

Early in the morning Phil checks in at the melon company. Farm trucks of freshly picked melons stand ready to be loaded onto the trailers. Loading usually takes three to four hours, and there are rigs ahead of his.

After lunch Phil is on line at the loading dock. Two other truckers help him to put sides on the trailer to receive the melons. Upright posts with grooves are fitted into niches on the floor of the truck. Large plywood boards are then slipped between them to form a container.

At loading time an open truck with melons pulls up beside the flatbed. Several men get into the rig and the melons are tossed from one truck to the other. One man arranges the melons in the flatbed. His job is the most difficult because the arranging must be done with extreme care. Fruit cannot be bruised. The melons must be evenly distributed on the flatbed for a smooth ride. Phil watches to see that everything is going well and then returns to the drivers' lounge.

The lounge is air-conditioned and has a telephone and a soda machine. The drivers are able to relax, sleep, and exchange stories. There is a small market nearby, and Phil brings back sandwich fixings for everyone.

Once the melons are packed, there is still paperwork to do. Phil doesn't leave Immokalee until 9:00 P.M. Sunday. He drives in the cool of the night and stops to sleep at dawn at a Perlis truck stop in Valdosta, Georgia.

Russell, a friend from Oneida who's also hauling melons to Toronto, pokes his head into the front of the truck and knocks on the window of the cab. The sun is high. "Hey, sleepyhead. It's me. Wake up and come 'n' eat."

"It's the middle of the night, you turkey," Phil jokes. But he puts on his boots and gets ready to go. It's always good to have company.

In the coffee shop Phil tells Russell that the truck has been making too much noise and is using too much fuel. He suspects that the engine may need to be tuned. When he gets home to Tennessee he will have the Kenworth people look at the engine while the tires are being changed.

The next day Phil is at the East Tennessee Tire Company in downtown Knoxville. Phil pulls in and spends the night. In the morning he disconnects the rig from the cab and is the first customer in the shop.

"The tires are loose laterally. There's erosion in the wheel assembly. Comes from wear and tear—just truckin'," a mechanic tells Phil.

"The front enders are gonna fix it best they can." The front enders are mechanics who only work on the front ends of trucks.

The men who fix the tires work as a team. One man removes the bolts. Another takes the tire. The next removes the rim, and yet another soaps the tire to look for damage.

After the tire is repaired, the team works in reverse. The rim is replaced, the tire rolled back and set into place, and the lug nuts are secured. It's orchestrated like a dance and no one misses a beat.

The Kenworth needs two new tires at three hundred dollars apiece. Phil also has to pay for repair and rotation, so the total bill for the tires is about seven hundred and fifty dollars.

Something about the truck doesn't sound right, but Phil doesn't know exactly what it is. The valves may need to be adjusted. He drives the cab into the machine shop.

With the engine turned on, several mechanics observe the rig and listen. "Too much smoke is coming out of the stacks. Too much fuel is being injected," one of the mechanics says.

They decide to check the engine and the fuel heaters first. They know that the tires, another possible cause for poor fuel economy, have just been rotated.

The head mechanic is explaining how the staff works to one of his new customers.

"We start with the simplest and most straightforward thing that could be wrong with the truck, and then we go from there. Nothing's more embarrassing than taking the whole thing apart and discovering that it was only a simple adjustment that had to be made."

The mechanics work on Phil's rig for an entire day and part of the evening. They find things that they don't like, but they make no firm diagnosis. Phil will return again after the load of melons is delivered to the warehouse in Toronto.

At the warehouse, workers remove the melons from the truck. The rig is weighed before the melons are unloaded and then again when it is empty. This is how the warehouse can tell how many pounds of melons are being bought.

Phil's load of melons pays three dollars per hundred pounds. Eighty thousand pounds. The load is heavier than Phil thought it would be.

The time in the repair shop has cost Phil hours on the road. He missed a weekend at home picking up the load in Immokalee. He doesn't want to miss another. It's time to get moving.

Back home in Oneida, Hillary's class has been talking about how we get the things that we have: food, clothing, toys, books, and all the other goods that we need to live. Her teacher has told the children that most things arrive by truck.

Phil and Hillary have come up with a plan. Hillary has asked her teacher if her dad can visit school with the truck. That Monday Phil brings the Kenworth into the parking lot of the Burchfield School. Then he goes inside to tell the principal that the truck is ready for company.

At first everyone seems afraid to get close. The truck is so large. The wheels are almost as tall as the tallest boy in the class. The fenders are as high as the corn that grows in the fields.

The children have always been cautioned: Stay away from traffic; Stay away from the big trucks; The highway is off-limits. But, of course, this is different. Yet they hesitate.

"Climb aboard. Take a good look," Phil says.

"Can we really go inside?" the children ask.

"Why, sure!" Phil answers.

"Can we sit at the wheel?"

"Of course you can! That's why I'm here with the truck."

"Can we get into the back bunk?" someone asks.

"And turn on the TV?" asks another.

"I don't see why not," Phil tells them.

Some of the braver children begin to try to climb into the cab. But, the cab is so high that they can barely reach it.

Time for Phil to lend a hand. "Anyone need a hitch up?" he asks. Soon the entire class, all twenty-three children, is in the truck.

Some are afraid that it might start to roll. Phil reassures them that it isn't possible for the truck to go anywhere or to start by itself.

"How about the keys?" someone asks as he settles himself behind the wheel. "I think I'll go for a spin."

After they have looked at everything, even under the hood, the children go back to their classroom. Phil comes in and sits down to talk.

"Anyone got any questions?" he asks. "Anything you want to know about the truck?"

There is a lot that the children want to know. Does Phil always wear snakeskin boots when he drives? How many miles does he drive each week? What kinds of loads does he pull? How much fuel does the truck use?

They all want to be truck drivers when they grow up.

"You're away from home a lot," says Phil. "It's a big responsibility."

Phil tells the class that most truck drivers are good drivers. They have to be, or they couldn't stay in business. But sometimes there are problems.

"Because a truck is so big, it can't make a short stop, especially if it's loaded," he explains. "It has to do with the weight-to-braking ratio. You've got to be very careful if you see a big rig coming along.

"Did you notice," Phil asks, "that when you are sitting at the wheel, you're so high up that you can't see the ground easily?

"Well, a driver might have trouble seeing you if you were down there right in front of him. You've got to remember to keep out of the way when you're on your bike or just walking along."

The children promise that they will remember.

When it's time to leave, Hillary goes outside, hugs her dad good-bye, and waves as she watches him leap up into the rig.

She knows just what he'll do to get the truck ready to roll. First, he revs the engine. Hillary listens, too. Yes, everything sounds okay for now. Then he checks the gauges. She closes her eyes and imagines the different dials spread out before her.

As Phil swings out onto the macadam headed for I-75, he waves to Hillary, honks the horn, and sends up puffs of smoke for luck.

Over the roar of the engine, Hillary shouts, "See you in five, old buddy."

One day I'll drive a big rig, too, she thinks as she returns to her classroom.